NĀGA-MANDALA
Play with a Cobra

Girish Karnad

*Translated from the original Kannada
by the author*

NĀGA-MANDALA

Play with a Cobra

GIRISH KARNAD
Translated from the Original Kannada
by the Author

DELHI
OXFORD UNIVERSITY PRESS
BOMBAY CALCUTTA MADRAS

Oxford University Press, Walton Street, Oxford OX2 6DP

OXFORD   NEW YORK   TORONTO
DELHI   BOMBAY   CALCUTTA   MADRAS   KARACHI
KUALA LUMPUR   SINGAPORE   HONG KONG   TOKYO
NAIROBI   DAR ES SALAAM   CAPE TOWN
MELBOURNE   AUCKLAND   MADRID
and associates in
BERLIN   IBADAN

ISBN 0 19 562622 2

Printed at Rekha Printers Pvt. Ltd., New Delhi 110020
and published by Neil O'Brien, Oxford University Press
YMCA Library Building, Jai Singh Road, New Delhi 110001

for
A. K. RAMANUJAN
friend, guru, hero

PREFACE

Nāga-Mandala is based on two oral tales from Karnataka which I first heard several years ago from Professor A. K. Ramanujan. But that is only the least of the reasons for dedicating this play to him.

I wrote *Nāga-Mandala* during the year I spent at the University of Chicago as Visiting Professor and Fulbright Scholar-in-Residence. I am most grateful to Professor Stuart M. Tave, Dean, Division of Humanities, and Professor C. M. Naim, Chairman, Department of South Asian Languages and Civilizations as well as to the Council for International Exchange of Scholars for having made that visit possible. I am further indebted to Professor Naim for persuading me to put the play into English.

I write in Kannada. English is the language of my adulthood. This translation must therefore be seen only as an approximation to the original. My deepest thanks are due to the colleagues and students who helped with the production of the play at the University Theater at Chicago, for their many valuable suggestions and textual corrections, as well as to Shri Shankar Nag who first presented the play in Kannada with his group, Sanket.

I am conscious that Naga's long speech on p. 25 owes much to Jean Anouilh, though I have not been able to identify the play.

Bombay   G. K.
28 November 1988

CHARACTERS
(*In the order of their appearance*)

THE MAN

THE FLAMES

THE STORY

RANI (*which means* QUEEN)

APPANNA (*which means* ANY MAN)

KURUDAVVA (*which means* THE BLIND ONE)

KAPPANNA (*which means* THE DARK ONE)

NAGA (*which means* THE COBRA)

THREE VILLAGE ELDERS

CROWDS

Appanna and Naga are played by the same actor.

PROLOGUE

(*The inner sanctum of a ruined temple. The idol is broken, so the presiding deity of the temple cannot be identified.*

It is night. Moonlight seeps in through the cracks in the roof and the walls.

A man is sitting in the temple. Long silence. Suddenly, he opens his eyes wide. Closes them. Then uses his fingers to pry open his eyelids. Then he goes back to his original morose stance.

He yawns involuntarily. Then reacts to the yawn by shaking his head violently, and turns to the audience.)

MAN: I may be dead within the next few hours.
   (*Long pause.*)
   I am not talking of 'acting' dead. Actually dead. I might die right in front of your eyes.
   (*Pause.*)
   A mendicant told me: 'You must keep awake at least one whole night this month. If you can do that, you'll live. If not, you will die on the last night of the month.' I laughed out loud when I heard him. I thought nothing would be easier than spending a night awake.
   (*Pause.*)
   I was wrong. Perhaps death makes one sleepy. Every night this month I have been dozing off before even being aware of it. I am convinced I am seeing something with these eyes of mine, only to wake up and find I was dreaming. Tonight is my last chance.
   (*Pause.*)
   For tonight is the last night of the month. Even of my life, perhaps? For how do I know sleep won't creep in on me again as it has every night so far? I may doze off right in front of you. And that will be the end of me.
   (*Pause.*)
   I asked the mendicant what I had done to deserve this fate. And he said: 'You have written plays. You have staged them.

You have caused so many good people, who came trusting you, to fall asleep twisted in miserable chairs, that all that abused mass of sleep has turned against you and become the Curse of Death.'

(*Pause.*)

I hadn't realized my plays had had that much impact.

(*Pause.*)

Tonight may be my last night. So I have fled from home and come to this temple, nameless and empty. For years I've been lording it over my family as a writer. I couldn't bring myself to die a writer's death in front of them.

(*Pause.*)

I swear by this absent God, if I survive this night I shall have nothing more to do with themes, plots or stories. I abjure all story-telling, all play-acting.

(*Female voices are heard outside the temple. He looks.*)

Voices! Here? At this time of night? Lights! Who could be coming here now?

(*He hides behind a pillar. Several Flames enter the temple, giggling, talking to each other in female voices.*)

MAN: I don't believe it! They are naked lamp flames! No wicks, no lamps. No one holding them. Just lamp flames on their own—floating in the air! Is that even possible?

(*Another three or four Flames enter, talking among themselves.*)

FLAME 3: (*Addressing Flame 1, which is already in the temple.*) Hello! What a pleasant surprise! You are here before us tonight.

FLAME 1: That master of our house, you know what a skinflint he is! He is convinced his wife has a hole in her palm, so he buys all the groceries himself. This evening, before the dark was even an hour old, they ran out of *kusbi* oil. The tin of peanut oil didn't go far. The bowl of castor oil was empty anyway. So they had to retire to bed early and I was permitted to come here.

(*Laughter.*)

FLAME 2: (*Sneering*) *Kusbi* oil! Peanut oil! How disgusting! My family comes from the coast. We won't touch anything but coconut oil.

FLAME 1: . . . But at least I come here every night. What about your friend, the kerosene flame? She hasn't been seen here for months. She is one of the first tonight.

FLAME 4: Actually, from today on I don't think I'll have any difficulty getting out . . . and early.

(*They all laugh.*)

FLAME 1: Why? What's happened?

(*The other Flames giggle.*)

FLAMES: Tell her! Tell her!

FLAME 4: My master had an old, ailing mother. Her stomach was bloated, her back covered with bed sores. The house stank of cough and phlegm, pus and urine. No one got a wink of sleep at night. Naturally, I stayed back too. The old lady died this morning, leaving behind my master and his young wife, young and juicy as a tender cucumber. I was chased out fast.

(*Giggles.*)

FLAME 3: You are lucky. My master's eyes have to feast on his wife limb by limb if the rest of him is to react. So we lamps have to bear witness to what is better left to the dark.

(*They all talk animatedly. New Flames come and join them. They group and regroup, chattering.*)

MAN: (*To the audience.*) I had heard that when lamps are put out in the village, the flames gather in some remote place and spend the night together, gossiping. So this is where they gather!

(*A new Flame enters and is enthusiastically greeted.*)

FLAME 1: You are late. It is well past midnight.

NEW FLAME: Ah! There was such a to-do in our house tonight.

FLAMES: What happened? Tell us!

NEW FLAME: You know I have only an old couple in my house. Tonight the old woman finished eating, swept and cleaned the floor, put away the pots and pans, and went to the room in which her husband was sleeping. And what should she see, but a young woman dressed in a rich, new sari step out of the room! The moment the young woman saw my mistress, she ran out of the house and disappeared into the night. The old woman woke her husband up and questioned him. But he said he knew nothing. Which started the rumpus.

FLAMES: But who was the young woman? How did she get into your house?

NEW FLAME: Let me explain: My mistress, the old woman, knows a story and a song. But all these years she has kept them to herself, never told the story, nor sung the song. So the story and the song were being choked, imprisoned inside her. This afternoon the old woman took her usual nap after lunch and started snoring. The moment her mouth opened, the story and the song jumped out and hid in the attic. At night, when the old man had gone to sleep, the story took the form of a young woman and the song became a sari. The young woman wrapped herself in the sari and stepped out, just as the old lady was coming in. Thus, the story and song created a feud in the family and were revenged on the old woman.

FLAME 1: So if you try to gag one story, another happens.

FLAMES: (*All together.*) But where are they now, the poor things? . . . How long will they run around in the dark? What will happen to them?

NEW FLAME: I saw them on my way here and told them to follow me. They should be here any moment. . . . There they are! The story with the song!

(*The Story, in the form of a woman dressed in a new, colourful sari, enters, acknowledges the enthusiastic welcome from the Flames with a languid wave of the hand and goes and sits in a corner, looking most despondent. The Flames gather around her.*)

NEW FLAME: Come on. Why are you so despondent? We are here and are free the whole night. We'll listen to you.

STORY: Thank you, my dears. It is kind of you. But what is the point of your listening to a story? You can't pass it on.

FLAMES: That's true. . . . What can we do? Wish we could help. (*While the Flames make sympathetic noises, the Man jumps out from behind the pillar and grabs the Story by her wrist.*)

MAN: I'll listen to you!

(*The Flames flee helter-skelter in terror. The Story struggles to free herself.*)

STORY: Who are you? Let me go!

MAN: What does it matter who I am, I'll listen to you. Isn't that enough? I promise you, I'll listen all night!

(*The Story stops struggling. There is a new interest in her voice.*)

STORY: You will?

MAN: Yes.

STORY: Good. Then let me go.

(*He does not.*) I need my hands to act out the parts.

(*He lets her go.*)

There is a condition, however—

MAN: What?

STORY: You can't just listen to the story and leave it at that. You must tell it again to someone else.

MAN: That I certainly shall, if I live. But first I must be alive to ... That reminds me. I have a condition, too.

STORY: Yes?

MAN: I must not doze off during the tale. If I do, I die. All your telling will be wasted.

STORY: As a self-respecting story, that is the least I can promise.

MAN: All right then. Start. (*Suddenly.*) But no! No! It's not possible. I take back my word. I can't repeat the story.

STORY: And why not?

MAN: I have just now taken a vow not to have anything to do with themes, plots or acting. If I live, I don't want to risk any more curses from the audience.

STORY: (*Gets up.*) Good-bye then. We must be going.

MAN: Wait! Don't go. Please.

(*Thinks.*)

I suppose I have no choice.

(*To the audience.*)

So now you know why this play is being done. I have no choice. Bear with me, please. As you can see, it is a matter of life and death for me.

(*Calls out.*)

Musicians, please!

(*Musicians enter and occupy their mat.*)

The Story and the Song!

(*Throughout the rest of the play, the Man and the Story remain on stage. The Flames too listen attentively though from a distance.*) (*To the Story.*) Go on.

ACT ONE

(The locked front door of a house with a yard in front of the house, and on the right, an enormous ant-hill. The interior of the house—the kitchen, the bathroom as well as Rani's room—is clearly seen.)

STORY: A young girl. Her name . . . it doesn't matter. But she was an only daughter, so her parents called her Rani. Queen. Queen of the whole wide world. Queen of the long tresses. For when her hair was tied up in a knot, it was as though a black King Cobra lay curled on the nape of her neck, coil upon glistening coil. When it hung loose, the tresses flowed, a torrent of black, along her young limbs, and got entangled in her silver anklets. Her fond father found her a suitable husband. The young man was rich and his parents were both dead. Rani continued to live with her parents until she reached womanhood. Soon, her husband came and took her with him to his village. His name was—well, any common name will do—

MAN: Appanna?

STORY: Appanna.

(Appanna enters, followed by Rani. They carry bundles in their arms, indicating that they have been travelling. Appanna opens the lock on the front door of the house. They go in.)

APPANNA: Have we brought in all the bundles?

RANI: Yes.

APPANNA: Well, then, I'll be back tomorrow at noon. Keep my lunch ready. I shall eat and go.

(Rani looks at him nonplussed. He pays no attention to her, goes out, shuts the door, locks it from outside and goes away. She runs to the door, pushes it, finds it locked, peers out of the barred window. He is gone.)

RANI: Listen—please—

(She does not know what is happening, stands perplexed. She cannot even weep. She goes and sits in a corner of her room.

*Talks to herself indistinctly. Her words become distinct as
the lights dim. It is night.)*

... So Rani asks him: 'Where are you taking me?' And the Eagle
answers: 'Beyond the seven seas and the seven isles. On the
seventh island is a magic garden. And in that garden stands the
tree of emeralds. Under that tree, your parents wait for you.'
So Rani says: 'Do they? Then please, please take me to them—
immediately. Here I come.' So the Eagle carries her clear across
the seven seas ...

*(She falls asleep. Moans 'Oh, Mother!' 'Father' in her sleep.
It gets light. She wakes up with a fright, looks around, then
runs to the bathroom, mimes splashing water on her face,
goes into the kitchen, starts cooking. Appanna comes. Opens
the lock on the front door and comes in. Goes to the
bathroom. Mimes bathing, then comes to the kitchen and sits
down to eat. She serves him food.)*

RANI: Listen—*(Fumbling for words)* Listen—I feel—
frightened—alone at night—

APPANNA: What is there to be scared of? Just keep to yourself.
No one will bother you. Rice!

(Pause.)

RANI: Please, you could—

APPANNA: Look, I don't like idle chatter. Do as you are told, you
understand?

(Finishes his meal, gets up.)

I'll be back tomorrow, for lunch.

*(Appanna washes his hands, locks her in and goes away.
Rani watches him blankly through the window.)*

STORY: And so the days rolled by.

*(Mechanically, Rani goes into the kitchen, starts cooking.
Talks to herself.)*

RANI: Then Rani's parents embrace her and cry. They kiss her
and caress her. At night she sleeps between them. So she is
not frightened any more. 'Don't worry,' they promise her.
'We won't let you go away again ever!' In the morning, the
stag with the golden antlers comes to the door. He calls out
to Rani. She refuses to go. 'I am not a stag,' he explains, 'I
am a prince' ...

(Rani sits staring blankly into the oven. Then begins to sob.

Outside, in the street, Kappanna enters, carrying Kurudavva on his shoulders. She is blind. He is in his early twenties.)

KAPPANNA: Mother, you can't do this! You can't start meddling in other people's affairs the first thing in the morning. That Appanna should have been born a wild beast or a reptile. By some mistake, he got human birth. He can't stand other people. Why do you want to tangle with him?

KURUDAVVA: Whatever he is, he is the son of my best friend. His mother and I were like sisters. Poor thing, she died bringing him into this world. Now a new daughter-in-law comes to her house. How can I go on as though nothing has happened? Besides, I haven't slept a wink since you told me you saw Appanna in his concubine's courtyard. He has got himself a bride—and he still goes after that harlot?

KAPPANNA: I knew I shouldn't have told you. Now you have insomnia—and I have a backache.

KURUDAVVA: Who's asked you to carry me around like this? I haven't, have I? I was born and brought up here. I can find my way around.

KAPPANNA: Do you know what I ask for when I pray to Lord Hanuman of the Gymnasium every morning? For more strength. Not to wrestle. Not to fight. Only so I can carry you around.

KURUDAVVA: (*Pleased*) I know, I know.
    (*Suddenly Kappanna freezes.*)
What is it? Why have you stopped?
    (*He doesn't answer. Merely stands immobile and stares. A touch of panic in Kurudavva's voice.*)
What is it, Kappanna? Kappanna!

KAPPANNA: Nothing, Mother. It's just that I can see Appanna's front door from here.

KURUDAVVA: (*Relieved*) Oh! For a moment I was worried it was that—who-is-that-again? That witch or fairy, whatever she is—who you say follows you around.

KAPPANNA: Mother, she is not a witch or a fairy. When I try to explain, you won't even listen. And then, when I'm not even thinking of her, you start suspecting all kinds of—

KURUDAVVA: Hush! Enough of her now. Tell me why we have stopped.

KAPPANNA: There doesn't seem to be anyone in Appanna's house. There is a lock on the front door.

KURUDAVVA: How is that possible? Even if he is lying in his concubine's house, his bride should be home.

KAPPANNA: Who can tell about Appanna? He's a lunatic . . .

KURUDAVVA: You don't think he could have sent his wife back to her parents already, do you? Come, let us look in through the window and check.

KAPPANNA: Of course not, Mother! If someone sees us—

KURUDAVVA: Listen to me. Go up to the house and peep in. Tell me what you see.

KAPPANNA: I refuse.

KURUDAVVA: (*Tearful*) I wouldn't have asked you if I had eyes. I don't know why God has been cruel to me, why he gave me no sight . . .

KAPPANNA: (*Yielding*) All right, Mother.
(*They go near the house. Kappanna peers through the window.*)

KAPPANNA: The house is empty.

KURUDAVVA: Of course it is, silly! How can anyone be inside when there is a lock outside on the door? Tell me, can you see clothes drying inside? What kind of clothes? Any saris? Skirts? Or is it only men's clothes?

KAPPANNA: I can't see a thing!

RANI: Who is it? What is that outside?

KAPPANNA: Oh my God!
(*Lifts Kurudavva and starts running.*)

KURUDAVVA: Stop! Stop, I tell you! Why are you running as though you've seen a ghost?

KAPPANNA: There is someone inside the house—a woman!

KURUDAVVA: You don't have to tell me that! So what if there is a woman inside the house? We have come here precisely because a woman is supposed to be in the house.

KAPPANNA: Mother, what does it mean when a man locks his wife in?

KURUDAVVA: You tell me.

KAPPANNA: It means he does not want anyone to talk to his wife.

RANI: (*Comes to the window.*) Who is it?

KAPPANNA: Let's go.

(*Starts running again. Kurudavva hits him on the back.*)

KURUDAVVA: Stop! Stop! (*To Rani*) I am coming, child! Right
now! Don't go away! (*To Kappana*) He keeps his wife locked
up like a caged bird? I must talk to her. Let me
down—instantly!

(*He lets her down.*)

You go home if you like.

KAPPANNA: I'll wait for you here under the tree. Come back
soon. Don't just sit there gossiping . . .

KURUDAVVA: (*Approaching Rani*) Dear girl . . .

RANI: Who are you?

KURUDAVVA: Don't be afraid. I am called Kurudavva, because I
am blind. Your mother-in-law and I were like sisters. I helped
when your husband was born. Don't be frightened. Appanna
is like a son to me. Is he not in?

RANI: No.

KURUDAVVA: What is your name?

RANI: They call me Rani.

KURUDAVVA: And where is Appanna?

RANI: I don't know.

KURUDAVVA: When did he go out?

RANI: After lunch yesterday.

KURUDAVVA: When will he come back?

RANI: He will be back for lunch later in the day.

KURUDAVVA: You don't mean, he is home only once a day, and
that too . . . only for lunch?

(*No reply.*)

And you are alone in the house all day?

(*Rani begins to sob.*)

Don't cry child, don't cry. I haven't come here to make you
cry. Does he lock you up every day like this?

RANI: Yes, since the day I came here . . .

KURUDAVVA: Does he beat you or ill-treat you?

RANI: No.

KURUDAVVA: (*Pause.*) Does he . . . 'talk' to you?

RANI: Oh, that he does. But not a syllable more than required.
'Do this', 'Do that', 'Serve the food.'

KURUDAVVA: You mean—? That means—you are—still—hmm!
Has he . . .?

RANI: Apart from him, you are the first person I have seen since coming here. I'm bored to death. There is no one to talk to!

KURUDAVVA: That's not what I meant by 'talk'. Has your husband touched you? How can I put it? (*Exasperated.*) Didn't anyone explain to you before your wedding? Your mother? Or an aunt?

RANI: Mother started shedding tears the day I matured and was still crying when I left with my husband. Poor her! She is probably crying even now.

   (*Starts sobbing.*)

KURUDAVVA: Dear girl, it's no use crying. Don't cry! Don't! Come here. Come, come to the window. Let me touch you. My eyes are all in my fingers.

   (*She feels Rani's face, shoulder, neck through the bars of the window.*)

Ayyo! How beautiful you are. Ears like hibiscus. Skin like young mango leaves. Lips like rolls of silk. How can that Appanna gallivant around leaving such loveliness wasting away at home?

RANI: I am so frightened at night, I can't sleep a wink. At home, I sleep between Father and Mother. But here, alone—Kurudavva, can you help me, please? Will you please send word to my parents that I am, like this, here? Will you ask them to free me and take me home? I would jump into a well—if only I could—

KURUDAVVA: Chih! Chih! You shouldn't say such things. I'll take care of everything.

   (*Calls out.*)

Son! Son!

KAPPANNA: (*From behind the tree.*) Yes?

KURUDAVVA: Come here.

KAPPANNA: No, I won't.

KURUDAVVA: Come here, you idiot.

KAPPANNA: I absolutely refuse, Mother. I told you right at the start that I won't.

KURUDAVVA: Honestly!

   (*Comes to him.*)

Listen, Son. Run home now. Go into the cattle shed—the left corner—

KAPPANNA: The left corner—

KURUDAVVA: Just above where you keep the plough, behind the
pillar, on the shelf—

KAPPANNA: Behind the pillar—on the shelf—

KURUDAVVA: There is an old tin trunk. Take it down. It's full of
odds and ends, but take out the bundle of cloth. Untie it.
Inside there is a wooden box.

KAPPANNA: A wooden box. All right—

KURUDAVVA: In the right hand side of the wooden box is a
coconut shell wrapped in a piece of paper. Inside are two
pieces of a root. Bring them.

KAPPANNA: Now?

KURUDAVVA: Now. At once. Before Appanna returns home.

KAPPANNA: Mother, listen to me. If he finds you here—

KURUDAVVA: Don't waste time now. Do as I say. Run.

(*Gets up and comes back to the house. Kappanna leaves.*)
Are you still there?

RANI: Yes. Who is that?

KURUDAVVA: My son, Kappanna. Oh, don't let his name mislead
you. He isn't really dark. In fact, when he was born, my
husband said: 'Such a fair child! Let's call him the Fair One!'
I said: 'I don't know what Fair means. My blind eyes know
only the dark. So let's call this little parrot of my eyes the
Dark One!' And he became Kappanna.

RANI: And where have you sent him?

KURUDAVVA: I'll tell you. I was born blind. No one would marry
me. My father wore himself out going from village to village
looking for a husband. But to no avail. One day a mendicant
came to our house. No one was home. I was alone. I looked
after him in every way. Cooked hot food specially for him and
served him to his heart's content. He was pleased with me
and gave me three pieces of a root. 'Any man who eats one of
these will marry you', he said.

RANI: And then?

KURUDAVVA: 'Feed him the smallest piece first', he said. 'If that
gives no results, then try the middle-sized one. Only if both
fail, feed him the largest piece.'

RANI: (*Entranced.*) And then?

KURUDAVVA: One day a boy distantly related to me came to our

village and stayed with us. That day I ground one of the
pieces into paste, mixed it in with the food, and served him.
Can you guess which piece I chose?

RANI: (*Working it out.*) Which one now? The smallest one, as
the mendicant said? No, no, surely the biggest piece.

KURUDAVVA: No. I was in such a hurry I barely noticed the
small one. The biggest scared me. So I used the middle-sized
root.

RANI: And then?

KURUDAVVA: He finished his meal, gave me one look and
instantly fell in love. Married me within the next two days.
Never went back to his village. It took the plague to detach
him from me.

    (*Rani laughs.*)

KAPPANNA: (*Entering.*) Mother—

KURUDAVVA: Ha! There he is! Wait!

    (*Goes to him.*)

Have you brought them?

    (*Kappanna gives her the two pieces of root. Kurudavva
    hurries back to Rani.*)

Are you still there?

RANI: Yes, I am.

KURUDAVVA: Here.

RANI: What is that?

KURUDDAVVA: The root I was telling you about.

    (*Rani starts.*) Here. Take this smaller piece. That should do
for a pretty jasmine like you. Take it! Grind it into a nice
paste and feed it to your husband and watch the results. Once he
smells you he won't go sniffing after that bitch. He will make you
a wife instantly.

RANI: But I am his wife already.

KURUDAVVA: Just do as I say.

    (*Rani takes the piece. Kurudavva tucks the other one in the
    knot of her sari. Kappanna whistles. She turns.*)

That must be Appanna coming.

RANI: (*Running in.*) Go now, Kurudavva. But come again.

KURUDAVVA: I shall too. But don't forget what I told you.

    (*Kurudavva starts to go. Appanna crosses her.*)

APPANNA: (*Suspicious*) Who is that? Kurudavva?

KURUDAVVA: How are you, Appanna? It's been a long time—

APPANNA: What are you doing here?

KURUDAVVA: I heard you had brought a new bride. Thought I would talk to her. But she refuses to come out.

APPANNA: She won't talk to any one. And no one need talk to her.

KURUDAVVA: If you say so.

> (*Exits.*)

APPANNA: (*So she can hear*) I put a lock on the door so those with sight could see. Now what does one do about blind meddlers? I think I'll keep a watch dog.

> (*Opens the door and goes in. To Rani.*)

I am lunching out today. I'll have my bath and go. Just heat up a glass of milk for me.

> (*Goes into the bathroom. Mimes bathing. Rani boils the milk. Pours it in a glass and starts to take it out. Notices the piece of root. Stops. Thinks. Runs out. Sees that he is still bathing. Runs back into the kitchen, makes a paste of the root.*)

APPANNA: (*Dressing*) Milk!

> (*Rani jumps with fright. Hurriedly mixes the paste into the milk. Comes out and gives Appanna the glass of milk. He drinks it in a single gulp. Hands the glass back to her. Goes to the door, ready to put the lock on. She watches him intently. He tries to shut the door. Suddenly clutches his head. Slides down to the floor. Stretches out and goes to sleep on the door-step, half inside and half outside the house. Rani is distraught. Runs to him. Shakes him. He doesn't wake up. He is in a deep sleep. She tries to drag him into the house, but he is too heavy for her. She sits down and starts crying.*)

APPANNA: (*Groggily*) Water! Water!

> (*She brings a pot of water. Splashes it on his face. He wakes up slowly, staggers up. Washes his face. Pushes her in. Locks the door from outside. Goes away. Rani watches, stunned. Slowly goes back to her bedroom. Starts talking to herself. It becomes night.*)

RANI: . . . . So the demon locks her up in his castle. Then it rains for seven days and seven nights. It pours. The sea floods

the city. The waters break down the door of the castle. Then
a big whale comes to Rani and says: 'Come, Rani, let us
go . . .'

> (*She falls asleep. Midnight. Kappanna enters carrying
> Kurudavva. Stumbles on a stone. They fall.*)

KURUDAVVA: Thoo! That's the problem with having eyes: one
can't see in the dark. That's why I have been telling you to let
me go on my own at least at night—

KAPPANNA: Go! Go! From this point on you can certainly go on
alone. I refuse to come any closer to that house. And what
are you doing, Mother? Suppose he is in the house. And he
hears you. What will you say? That you have come to gossip
with his wife in the dead of night?

KURUDAVVA: Shut up! We are here only to find out if the lock is
gone yet. If it's gone, he is inside now. That means success is
ours. We'll leave right away.

> (*Goes and touches the door. It is closed. Tip-toes to feel the
> latch. The lock is still there. Recoils in surprise.*)

I can't believe it. The lock is still there! (*Thinks.*)
Perhaps he has taken her out to the fields or the garden!
(*Laughs.*)

RANI: (*Wakes up.*) Who is that?

KURUDAVVA: Me.

RANI: (*Comes running.*) Who? Kurudavva? This time of the
night?

KURUDAVVA: What happened, child? Why is the lock still there?
(*No reply.*)
Did you feed him the root?

RANI: Yes.

KURUDAVVA: And what happened?

RANI: Nothing. He felt giddy. Fainted. Then got up and left.

KURUDAVVA: That's bad. This is no ordinary infatuation then.
That concubine of his is obviously—

RANI: Who?

KURUDAVVA: Didn't want to tell you. There is a woman, a bazaar
woman. She has your husband in her clutches. Squeezes him
dry. Maybe she's cast a spell. There is only one solution to
this—

RANI: What?

KURUDAVVA: (*Giving her the bigger piece.*) Feed him this larger piece of root.

RANI: No!

KURUDAVVA: Yes!

RANI: That little piece made him sick. This one—

KURUDAVVA: It will do good, believe me. This is not hearsay. I am telling you from my own experience. Go in. Start grinding it. Make a tasty curry. Mix the paste in it. Let him taste a spoonful and he will be your slave. And then? Just say the word and he will carry you to my house himself.

(*Rani blushes.*)

Son! Son!

(*To Rani.*) Remember. Don't let anything frighten you.

(*Rani goes into the kitchen. Kurudavva wakes up Kappanna. They exit. It gets brighter. Appanna comes. He has a vicious-looking dog on a chain with him. He brings it to the front yard and ties it to a tree stump there. Then comes to the front door and unlocks it. The dog begins to bark. Surprised at the bark, Rani peers out of the window.*)

RANI: Oh! A dog—

APPANNA: That blind woman and her son! Let them step here again and they'll know—! I'll bathe and come to eat. Serve my food.

(*Goes to the bathroom and starts bathing. Rani takes down her pot of curry. Removes the lid. Takes out the paste of the root.*)

RANI: (*To the Story.*) Shall I pour it in?

STORY: Yes. (*Continuing the narration*) So Rani prayed silently to the gods and poured the paste into the curry. There was an explosion. The curry turned red—blood red. Steam, pink and furious, enveloped Rani.

(*Rani mimes the entire action. Appanna calmly continues his bath. It is evident he has heard nothing.*)

RANI: Oh my god! What horrible mess is this? Blood. Perhaps poison. Shall I serve him this? That woman is blind, but he isn't. How could he possibly not see this boiling blood, this poisonous red? And then—even if he doesn't see it—how do I know it is not dangerous? Suppose something happens to

my husband? What will my fate be? That little piece made
him ill. Who knows . . .?

(*Slaps herself on her cheeks.*)

No, no. Forgive me, God. This is evil. I was about to commit
a crime. Father, Mother, how could I, your daughter, agree to
such a heinous act? No, I must get rid of this before he
notices anything.

(*She brings the pot out. Avoids the husband in the
bathroom. Steps out of the house. Starts pouring out the
curry. Stops.*)

RANI: No! How awful! It's leaving a red stain. He is bound to
notice it, right here on the door-step! What shall I do?
Where can I pour it, so he won't see?

STORY: Rani, put it in that ant-hill.

RANI: Ah, the ant-hill!

(*Runs to the tall ant-hill. Starts pouring the liquid into it.
The dog starts howling in the front yard.*)

APPANNA: Rani! See what is bothering the dog!

(*Surprised at receiving no reply.*) Rani! Rani!

(*Goes to the kitchen, drying himself. She is not there. Comes
to the front door looking for her. By this time Rani has
poured the curry into the ant-hill and is running back to the
house. The moment she turns her back to the ant-hill, a
King Cobra lifts its hood, hissing, out of the ant-hill. Looks
around. It sees Rani and follows her at a distance. By the
time she has reached the front door of her house, it is behind
a nearby tree, watching her.*

*Rani comes to the front door and freezes. Appanna is
waiting for her.*)

APPANNA: Rani, where have you been?

(*No answer.*)

I said, where have you been? Rani, answer me!

(*Moves aside so she can go in. But the moment she steps in,
Appanna slaps her hard. Rani collapses to the floor. He does
not look at her again. Just pulls the door shut, locks it from
outside and goes away. There is not a trace of anger in
anything he does. Just cold contempt. The dog barks loudly
at the King Cobra which watches from behind the tree,
hissing, excited, restless. Appanna goes away. Rani goes to*

her bedroom. Throws herself down in her usual corner,
crying.

It gets dark.

The King Cobra is still watching from under the tree. The
dog continues to bark.

When it is totally dark, the Cobra moves toward the
house. The barking becomes louder, more continuous. Rani
wakes up, goes to the window, curses and shouts. Goes back
to bed. The Cobra enters the house through the drain in the
bathroom.)

STORY: As you know, a cobra can assume any form it likes.
That night, it entered the house through the bathroom drain
and took the shape of—

(*The Cobra takes the shape of Appanna. To distinguish this*
Appanna from the real one, we shall call him Naga, meaning
a 'Cobra'.

Naga searches for Rani in the house. Finds her sleeping in
the bedroom. Watches her.)

ACT TWO

(Rani is sleeping and Naga is watching her from a distance, exactly as at the end of ACT ONE. *He moves nearer her and then gently caresses her. She wakes up with a start.)*

RANI: You—you—

NAGA: Don't get up.

RANI: But, when did you come? Shall I serve the food?

NAGA: *(Laughs.)* Food? At midnight?

RANI: Then something else. Perhaps—
  (Doesn't know what to say. Stands dazed, leaning against the wall.)

NAGA: Why don't you sit? Are you so afraid of me?
  (She shakes her head.)
  Then sit down.

RANI: No.

NAGA: I will go and sit there. Away from you. Will you at least sit then?
  (Moves away, sits on the floor at a distance from her.)
  Now?
  (Rani sits on the edge of the bed. Long silence. She is dozing but struggles to keep her eyes open.)

NAGA: You are very beautiful.

RANI: *(Startled.)* Hm? What? Do you—want something?

NAGA: No. I said you are very beautiful. Poor thing!

RANI: Poor thing—?

NAGA: That a tender bud like you should get such a rotten husband.

RANI: I didn't say anything!

NAGA: You didn't. I am saying it. Did it hurt . . . the beating this morning?

RANI: No.

NAGA: Locked up in the house all day. . . . You must be missing your parents.

RANI: (*Struggles to hold back a sob.*) No.

NAGA: They doted on you, didn't they?

(*She suddenly bursts out into a fit of weeping.*)

NAGA: (*Startled*) What is it?

(*Rani continues to howl.*)

I know, you want to see your parents, don't you? All right. I'll arrange that.

(*She looks at him dumbfounded.*)

Truly. Now, smile. Just a bit. Look, I'll send you to them only if you smile now.

(*Rani tries to smile. A new outburst of barking from the dog.*)

Oh! Does this dog carry on like that all night? How long is it since you had a good night's sleep?

RANI: But—

NAGA: (*Happy to see her react.*) But what?

RANI: Nothing.

NAGA: (*In order to provoke her.*) Listen to that racket! Have you had even one good night's sleep since coming here?

RANI: But—

NAGA: What are you 'but'ting about? But what?

RANI: But you brought the dog here only this morning! There was no problem all these days.

NAGA: (*Trying to cover up.*) Yes, of course.

RANI: Till this morning, once the housework was over . . . what was there to do? I used to sleep through the day and lie awake at night. Today this wretched dog has been barking away since it was brought here. That's why I was dozing when you came in. I'm sorry—

NAGA: (*Teasing*) Quite right! That won't do any more. From tomorrow I want you to be fresh and bright when I come home at night—

RANI: (*Uncertain*) At night?

NAGA: Yes. I shall come home every night from now on. May I?

(*Rani laughs shyly. Pause. She is sleepy.*)

May I sit by you now? Or will that make you jump out of your skin again?

(*Rani shakes her head. Naga comes and sits very close to her. When she tries to move away, he suddenly grabs her, with frightening speed.*)

NAGA: Don't be afraid. Put your head against my shoulder.
(*She slowly puts her head on his shoulder. He gently puts his arm around her.*)

NAGA: Now, don't be silly. I am not a mongoose or a hawk that you should be so afraid of me. Good. Relax. Tell me about your parents. What did all of you talk about? Did they pamper you? Tell me everything—
(*She has fallen asleep against his chest. He slowly unties her hair. It is long and thick and covers them both. He picks up her hair in his hand, smells it.*)

NAGA: What beautiful, long hair! Like dark, black, snake princesses!
(*He lays her down gently. Gets up. Goes to the bathroom, turns into his original self and slithers away. Morning. Rani wakes up, and looks around. No husband. Comes to the front door. Pushes it. It is still locked. Baffled, she washes her face, goes to the kitchen and starts cooking.*
The dog starts barking. Appanna comes. Pats the dog.)

APPANNA: Hello, friend! No intruders tonight, eh?
(*He unlocks the door and steps in. At the noise of the door, Rani comes out running. She is laughing.*)

RANI: But when did you go away? I'm . . .
(*Freezes when she sees the expression of distaste on his face.*)

APPANNA: Yes?

RANI: Oh! Nothing.

APPANNA: Good.
(*Goes to the bathroom. Rani stares after him, then returns to the kitchen.*)

RANI: I must have been dreaming again—
(*Appanna bathes, then eats silently as usual and leaves. It grows dark. Night. Rani lies in bed, wide awake. A long silence. The Cobra comes out of the ant-hill and enters the darkened front yard of her house. The dog suddenly begins to bark. Then, sounds of the dog growling and fighting, mixed with the hiss of a snake. The racket ends when the dog gives a long, painful howl and goes silent. Rani rushes to the window to see what is happening. It is dark. She cannot see anything. When silence is restored, she returns to her bed.*

*The Cobra enters the house through the drain and
becomes Naga. In the bathroom, he washes blood off his
cheeks and shoulder and goes to Rani's room. When she
hears his step on the stairs, she covers her head with the
sheet. Naga comes, sees her, smiles, sits on the edge of
her bed. Waits. She peeps out, sees him, closes her eyes
tight.)*

NAGA: What nonsense is this?

  (*Without opening her eyes, Rani bites her forefinger. Gives a
  cry of pain.*)

  What is going on, Rani?

RANI: (*Rubbing her finger.*) I must be going mad.

NAGA: Why?

RANI: (*To herself.*) His visit last night—I assumed I must have
dreamt that. I am certainly not dreaming now. Which means I
am going mad. Spending the whole day by myself is rotting
my brain.

NAGA: It is not a dream. I am not a figment of your imagination
either. I am here. I am sitting in front of you. Touch me.
Come on! You won't? Well, then. Talk to me. No? All right.
Then I had better go.

RANI: Don't. Please.

NAGA: What is the point of sitting silent like a stone image?

RANI: What do you—want me to say?

NAGA: Anything. Tell me about yourself. About your parents.
Whatever comes into your head. If you want me to stay, tell
me why. If you want me to go, say why.

RANI: (*Pouting.*) What can I say if you behave like this?

NAGA: Like what?

RANI: You talk so nicely at night. But during the day I only have
to open my mouth and you hiss like a . . . stupid snake.

  (*Naga laughs.*)

  It's all very well for you to laugh. I feel like crying.

NAGA: What should I do then—stop coming at night? Or
during the day?

RANI: Who am I to tell you that? It's your house. Your pleasure.

NAGA: No, let's say, the husband decides on the day visits. And
the wife decides on the night visits. So I won't come at night
if you don't want me to.

RANI: (*Eyes filling up.*) Why do you tease me like this? I am sick
of being alone. And then tonight, I was terrified you might
not come—that what I remembered from last night may be
just a dream. I was desperate that you should come again
tonight. But, what am I to say if you spin riddles like this?

NAGA: (*Seriously.*) I am afraid that is how it is going to be.
Like *that* during the day. Like *this* at night. Don't ask me
why.

RANI: I won't.

NAGA: Come. You slept like a child in my arms last night. You
must be sleepy now. Come. Go to sleep.

RANI: (*Moves into his arms, suddenly stops.*) But, what is this?
(*Touches his cheek.*)
Blood on your cheeks! And your shoulders! That looks like
tooth-marks. Did you run into a thorn bush or a barbed-wire
fence on your way here?

NAGA: Don't worry about it.

RANI: Wait. Let me apply that ointment Mother gave me. Where
is it? I took it out the other day when I cut my thumb slicing
onions. Where did I put it? Oh, yes! The mirror-box!
(*She rushes to the mirror-box and opens it. Before Naga can
move away so Rani won't see his reflection, she looks at him
in the mirror. Screams in fright. He moves with lightening
speed, pulls her away from the mirror and holds her in his
arms. She is trembling.*)

NAGA: What is it? What is it, Rani?
(*He gently shuts the mirror-box and pushes it away. Rani
turns and looks at where he had been sitting.*)

RANI: When I looked in the mirror, I saw there—where you
were sitting—instead of you, I saw a—
(*Mimes a cobra hood with her fingers.*)
—sitting there.

NAGA: What? A cobra?

RANI: (*Silencing him.*) Shh! Don't mention it. They say that if
you mention it by name at night, it comes into the house.

NAGA: All right. Suppose a cobra does come into this
house . . .

RANI: Don't! Why are you tempting fate by calling that
unmentionable thing by its name?

NAGA: . . . why shouldn't it come with love?

RANI: May God bless our house and spare us that calamity. The very thought makes me shudder.

NAGA: I am here now. Nothing more to fear.

(*They sit on the bed together.*)

RANI: Oh no! What am I to do with myself? In all this, I forgot to put the ointment on your wounds.

(*She tries to get up. He forces her down. She gently touches his wounds. Shivers.*)

Your blood is so cold. It's the way you wander about day and night heedless of wind and rain—

(*Stares into his eyes. Suddenly shuts her eyes and clasps him.*)

NAGA: What is it now?

RANI: (*Looking up.*) Since I looked into the mirror I seem to be incapable of thinking of anything else. Father says: 'If a bird so much as looks at a cobra—'

NAGA: There! Now you said 'cobra'. Now he is bound to come—

(*He mimes a cobra's hood with his hand.*)

RANI: Let it. I don't feel afraid anymore, with you beside me. Father says: 'The cobra simply hooks the bird's eyes with its own sight. The bird stares—and stares—unable to move its eyes. It doesn't feel any fear either. It stands fascinated, watching the changing colours in the eyes of the cobra. It just stares, its wings half-opened as though it was sculpted in the sunlight.'

NAGA: Then the snake strikes and swallows the bird.

(*He kisses her. They freeze. The Flames surround them and sing the song of the Flames (see p. 30). Rani gets up and goes and sits in a corner hiding her face behind her knees, her arms wrapped around her legs.*)

NAGA: What is it now?

RANI: Go away! Don't talk to me.

NAGA: But why are you crying?

RANI: I said be quiet.

(*Pause.*)

I didn't know you were such a bad man. I should have known the moment you started using honeyed words.

(*Pause.*)
Had I known, I would never have agreed to marry you. What will Father and Mother say if they come to know?

NAGA: They will say: 'Good! Our daughter is following nicely in our footsteps—'

RANI: (*Exploding.*) Quiet! I warn you, I am your wife and you don't have to answer anyone about me. But I will not have you say such things about my parents. They are not like—like—like dogs!

NAGA: (*Laughs.*) What have dogs done to deserve sole credit for it, you silly goose? Frogs croaking in pelting rain, tortoises singing soundlessly in the dark, foxes, crabs, ants, rattlers, sharks, swallows—even the geese! The female begins to smell like the wet earth. And stung by her smell, the King Cobra starts searching for his Queen. The tiger bellows for his mate. When the flame of forest blossoms into a fountain of red and the earth cracks open at the touch of the aerial roots of the banyan, it moves in the hollow of the cottonwood, in the flow of the estuary, the dark limestone caves from the womb of the heavens to the dark netherworlds, within everything that sprouts, grows, stretches, creaks and blooms—everywhere, those who come together, cling, fall apart lazily! It is there and there and there, everywhere.

RANI: Goodness! Goats have to be sacrificed and buffaloes slaughtered to get a word out of you in the mornings. But at night—how you talk! Snakes and lizards may do what they like, but human beings should have some sense of shame.

NAGA: (*Suddenly looks out.*) It is almost dawn. I must go.

RANI: No! No!

NAGA: The birds. Listen!

RANI: Why don't those birds choke on their own songs? Who has given them the right to mess about with other creatures' nights?

NAGA: I'll be back again at night.

RANI: Only at night? Not for lunch?

NAGA: Of course. There's always that. (*Pause.*) Listen, Rani. I shall come home every day twice. At night and of course again at mid-day. At night, wait for me here in this room. When I come and go at night, don't go out of this room, don't

look out of the window—whatever the reason. And don't ask
me why.

RANI: No, I won't. The pig, the whale, the eagle—none of them
asks why. So I won't either. But they ask for it again. So I can
too, can't I?

(*Runs to him and embraces him.*)

(*While the above scene is in progress, Kurudavva and
Kappanna have arrived outside. As usual, he lowers her to
the ground and sits under the tree. She goes to the door.
Stumbles over the dog. Surprised, she feels it, makes sure it
is dead. Feels the lock on the door. Calls out in a whisper.*)

KURUDAVVA: Kappanna!

KAPPANNA: Yes.

KURUDAVVA: Come here.

KAPPANNA: No, I won't.

KURUDAVVA: I said come here. This fool doesn't understand a
thing. Quick. Something funny is happening here.

(*Reluctantly, Kappanna comes to the door.*)

Look here.

KAPPANNA: A dog. And it is dead!

KURUDAVVA: It wasn't here the night before. And the lock is still
there. I wonder what the silly girl has gone and done. Look
inside the house. Can you see anything?

KAPPANNA: (*Looking*) No!

KURUDAVVA: Listen.

(*They listen. Naga walks toward the bathroom.*)

KAPPANNA: Footsteps.

KURUDAVVA: It's a man.

KAPPANNA: Appanna! He is inside. He will be out any minute!

KURUDAVVA: He can't! What about the lock? (*Thinks.*) And if
Appanna locked the door from the outside, who is in there
now? Look, look. See who it is.

KAPPANNA: I can't see anything from here.

KURUDAVVA: Try the window at the back.

(*Reluctantly he goes to the backyard. Naga goes to the
bathroom, turns into a King Cobra and goes out of the
drain, just as Kappanna arrives at the spot and sees the
Cobra emerge.*)

KAPPANNA: (*Screams.*) Snake! Snake! A cobra!

(*Rushes to the front door, picks up Kurudavva and starts to run.*)

KURUDAVVA: Where?

KAPPANNA: In the backyard! Out of the bathroom drain!

KURUDAVVA: Then why are you running? It isn't following us, is it? It should be gone by now. Let me down! Let me down!

(*Rani hears the commotion, comes running to the front door.*)

RANI: Who is it? Kurudavva?

KURUDAVVA: Let me down! Yes, it's me, child.

(*Comes back to the door.*)

KAPPANNA: Don't go too near, Mother. It may still be there—

RANI: What is it, Kurudavva? Who was that shouting?

KURUDAVVA: I won't come any closer. I'll speak from here. Kappanna says he saw a cobra there.

RANI: Where?

KURUDAVVA: Coming out of your bathroom drain.

RANI: Oh my God! I hope he didn't go to the bathroom—

(*Rushes to the bathroom, calling out to Appanna.*)

KURUDAVVA: Who do you mean? Appanna?

RANI: Yes.

(*She is relieved to find the bathroom empty. Comes back to the front door.*) He is not there. I told you—he left just a few minutes ago.

KURUDAVVA: We have been here the last half hour. No one has come out.

RANI: He certainly isn't in the house!

(*Pushes the door.*)

There! The door is locked from the outside. It wouldn't be if he was in here, would it? Perhaps you didn't see him come out?

KURUDAVVA: Maybe so. Well, my child, have you started your married life?

RANI: (*Blushing*) Yes, Kurudavva.

(*Yawns.*)

KURUDAVVA: (*Laughs*) Tired? Poor thing! So you see the power of my root? Didn't I tell you your husband will cling to you once he tastes it?

(*Rani embarrassed, tries to laugh.*)

KURUDAVVA: Well, my work is done. I'll be off now. Bless you.
Burn incense in a ladle and stick it into the drain. Keeps the
reptiles out.

RANI: Please come again.

(*Kappanna lifts up Kurudavva: They talk in whispers.*)

KAPPANNA: If the steps we heard were Appanna's, well, he
certainly hasn't come out of the house.

KURUDAVVA: Of course, he is in there. Once couples start
playing games, they begin to invent some pretty strange ones.
Come on. Let's go.

(*They move. Rani thinks for a while, goes into the bedroom.
Kappanna, carrying Kurudavva, suddenly stiffens. Stands
frozen, staring at something in the distance.*)

KURUDAVVA: Kappanna—Kappanna—

(*He does not respond. She hits him on his back in an effort
to wake him up. But he is immobile.*)

KURUDAVVA: (*Panicky*) Kappanna! What is it? Why do you act
like this? Kappanna—

(*He suddenly wakes up.*)

KAPPANNA: Eh? Nothing.

KURUDAVVA: What do you mean nothing? Giving me a scare like
that—

KAPPANNA: You won't believe me if I tell you. It was her
again—

KURUDAVVA: Why shouldn't I believe you if you talked sense?
Just admit it's one of the girls from a nearby village, instead
of making up fancy stories about some—

KAPPANNA: She is not a village girl. Which village girl will dare
step out at this hour? And I am not making up stories. That
day she floated out from the haunted well. Just now she
stepped out of the cemetery. Looked at me. Smiled and
waved.

KURUDAVVA: Perhaps she is an ogress. Of demon birth. Or
someone from the netherworld, perhaps. A spirit. Why don't
you just say who it is—

KAPPANNA: You won't let me—

KURUDAVVA: When you talk like this I feel we are falling apart.
It's a fear I have never felt before.

KAPPANNA: Mother, just listen—

KURUDAVVA: Shut up now!

> (*They exit, arguing: It gets brighter. It is mid-day. Appanna enters. Sees the dead dog.*)

APPANNA: What's wrong with this dog? Why is it asleep in the hot sun?

> (*Whistles. Then comes nearer and inspects.*)

It is dead! Dead! I paid fifty rupees for it!

> (*Rani comes to the front window and looks out.*)

APPANNA: Something has bitten it. Perhaps that cobra—from that ant-hill . . .

(*To Rani*) This was no ordinary hound. It cornered a cheetah once. It must have sensed the cobra. It must have given a fight. Didn't you hear anything at night?

> (*She shakes her head. He gets up.*)

APPANNA: I'd better go and find an Untouchable to bury the carcass.

> (*Appanna exits. Rani stares after him nonplussed. Touches herself on her cheek.*)

RANI: But last night . . . he had blood on his cheeks . . . and shoulders. Now . . .

> (*Goes to the kitchen. Starts cooking. Appanna comes, bathes, sits down to eat. She serves him food. He gets up. Locks the door and goes away.*)
>
> *While all this is going on, the story narrates the following.*)

STORY: The death of the dog infuriated Appanna. He next brought a mongoose. The mongoose lasted only one day. But it had evidently given a tougher fight: its mouth was full of blood. There were bits of flesh under its claws. Bits of snakeskin were found in its teeth.

Rani fainted when she saw the dead mongoose. That night he did not visit her. There was no sign of him the next fifteen days. Rani spent her nights crying, wailing, pining for him. When he started coming again, his body was covered with wounds which had only partly healed. She applied her ointment to the wounds, tended him. But she never questioned him about them. It was enough that he had returned. Needless to say, when her husband came during the day, there were no scars on him.

*(It gets dark on stage. Rani hurriedly lights the lamps in the
house. As she does so, some of the Flames get into position.)*

RANI: *(to the Flames)* Wait now. Don't be impatient. It won't be
long. . . . It will open out. Reach out with its fragrance.

*(Rushes into her bedroom. Waits tensely. Suddenly jumps
up, breathes in deeply.)*

RANI: There it is . . . **The smell of the blossoming nightqueen!**
How it fills the house before he comes! How it welcomes
him! God, how it takes me, sets each fibre in me on fire!

*(Naga comes, they embrace. The Flames surround them and
sing. Naga and Rani dance.)*

SONG OF THE FLAMES

*Come let us dance
   through the weaver-bird's nest
   and light the hanging lamps
   of glow-worms
   through the caverns in the ant-hill
   and set the diamond
   in the cobra's crown ablaze
   through the blind woman's dream
   through the deaf-mute's song
Come let us flow
   down the tresses of time
   all light and song.*

*(It is night. Rani and Naga are in bed together. Naga plays
with her loose hair. She suddenly laughs.)*

NAGA: What is it?

RANI: Thank God.

NAGA: Why?

RANI: All these days I was never sure I didn't just dream up
these nightly visits of yours. You don't know how I have
suffered. When I saw your scowling face in the mornings, I
would be certain everything was a fantasy and almost want to
cry. But my real anxiety began as the evening approached. I
would merely lie here, my eyes shut tight. What is there to
see after all? The same walls. The same roof. As the afternoon
passed my whole being got focused in my ears. The bells of
cattle returning home—that means it is late afternoon. The

cacophony of birds in a far-away tree—it is sunset. The chorus of crickets spreading from one grove to another—it is night. Now he will come. Suppose he doesn't tonight? Suppose the nightqueen bush does not blossom? Suppose it's all a dream? Every night the same anxiety. The same cold feeling deep within me! Thank God. That's all past now.

NAGA: Why?

RANI: I have definite evidence to prove I was not fantasizing.

NAGA: What evidence?

RANI: I am pregnant.

(*He stares at her, dumbfounded.*)

Why are you looking at me like that? There is a baby in my womb.

(*He stares blankly.*)

We are going to have a baby.

(*Pause.*)

It doesn't make you happy?

(*Anguished.* **What am I going to do with you? Laugh? Cry? Bang my head against the wall? I can never guess how you'll react. I thought you would dance with joy on hearing the news. That you would whirl me around and fondle me. Feel my stomach gently and kiss me. All that—**

(*Pause.*)

Actually, I was also afraid you might not do anything of that sort. That's why I hid the news from you all these months. I can't make any sense of you even when it is just the two of us. Now a third life joins us! I didn't know if that would be too much for you. So I was silent.

(*Her eyes fill up.*)

What I feared has come true. What kept me silent has happened. You are not happy about the baby. You are not proud that I am going to be a mother. Sometimes you are so cold-blooded—you cannot be human.

(*Forcibly puts his hand on her belly.*)

Just feel! Feel! Our baby is crouching in there, in the darkness, listening to the sounds from the world outside—as I do all day long.

NAGA: (*Dully*) I am glad you hid the news from me all this time.

Even now, try to keep from speaking about it as long as possible. Keep it a secret.

RANI: From whom?

NAGA: From me.

RANI: What are you talking about? I have already told you. How can it be a secret again? And how long can it remain a secret? Another fifteen days? Three weeks?

NAGA: (*Sadly*) I realize it cannot remain a secret for long. That is why I said, as long as possible. Please, do as I tell you.

RANI: (*Blankly*) Yes, I shall. Don't ask questions. Do as I tell you. Don't ask questions. Do as I tell you. No. I won't ask questions. I shall do what you tell me. Scowls in the day. Embraces at night. The face in the morning unrelated to the touch at night. But day or night, one motto does not change: Don't ask questions. Do as I tell you.

(*He is silent.*)

I was a stupid, ignorant girl when you brought me here. But now I am a woman, a wife, and I am going to be a mother. I am not a parrot. Not a cat or a sparrow. Why don't you take it on trust that I have a mind and explain this charade to me? Why do you play these games? Why do you change like a chameleon from day to night? Even if I understood a little, a tiny bit—I could bear it. But now—sometimes I feel my head is going to burst!

(*Naga opens his mouth to say something.*)

RANI: I know. Don't ask questions. Do as I say.

NAGA: (*Laughs.*) That is not what I was going to say.

RANI: You don't want the child, do you? If I had remained barren, I could have spent my whole life happily trying to work out whether all of this was real or a dream. But this is no dream now. Dreams remain in heads. This one has sent roots deep down into my womb.

(*Suddenly.*)

What shall I do? Shall I have an abortion?

(*Naga stares, blankly.*)

I may find a sharp instrument in the kitchen—a ladle, a knife. Or I can ask Kurudavva's help. No, it's too late. It is five months old. Too big to be kept a secret. Forgive me. I know it's *my* fault. But the secret will be out whatever I do.

NAGA: It's almost morning. I must go.

RANI: (*Waking up.*) What?

NAGA: I have to go.

RANI: (*Gently.*) Go.

(*She turns away. Naga takes a step to go. They both freeze. The lights change sharply from night to mid-day. In a flash, Naga becomes Appanna: Pushes her to the floor and kicks her.*)

APPANNA: Aren't you ashamed to admit it, you harlot? I locked you in, and yet you managed to find a lover! Tell me who it is. Who did you go to with your sari off?

RANI: I swear to you I haven't done anything wrong!

APPANNA: You haven't? And yet you have a bloated tummy. Just pumped air into it, did you? And you think I'll let you get away with that? You shame me in front of the whole village, you darken my face, you slut—!

(*He beats her. The Cobra watches this through a window and moves about, frantic. Neither notices it.*)

APPANNA: I swear to you I am not my father's son, if I don't abort that bastard! Smash it into dust! Right now—

(*Drags her into the street. Picks up a huge stone to throw on her. The Cobra moves forward, hissing loudly, drawing attention to itself. Rani screams.*)

RANI: Oh my God! A snake! A cobra!

(*Appanna throws the stone at the Cobra which instantly withdraws. Rani uses this moment to run into the house and lock herself in. Appanna runs behind her and bangs on the door.*)

APPANNA: Open the door! Open the door, you whore! All right then, I'll show you. I'll go to the Village Elders. If they don't throw that child into boiling oil and you along with it, my name is not Appanna.

(*He exits. She rushes to her bedroom. Lights change to night. She is crying on the floor. Naga comes and sits glumly nearby.*)

RANI: Why are you humiliating me like this? Why are you stripping me naked in front of the whole village? Why don't you kill me instead? I would have killed myself. But there's not even a rope in this house for me to use.

NAGA: Rani, the Village Elders will sit in judgement. You will be summoned. That cannot be avoided.

RANI: Look at the way you talk—as if you were referring to someone else. After all, you complained to the Elders about me. Now you can go and withdraw the complaint. Say my wife isn't a whore.

NAGA: **I'm sorry, but it can't be done. Rani, listen. You do** trust me, don't you?

RANI: You ask me that? Isn't all this a result of trusting you? (*Suddenly helpless.*) Who else is there for me?

NAGA: Then listen to me carefully. When you face the Elders, tell them you will prove your innocence. Say you will undertake the snake ordeal.

RANI: Snake ordeal? What is that?

NAGA: There is an enormous ant-hill under the banyan tree. Almost like a mountain. A King Cobra lives in it. Say you will put your hand into the ant-hill—

RANI: (*Screams.*) What?

NAGA: Yes. And pull out the King Cobra. And take your oath by that cobra.

RANI: I can't! I can't!

NAGA: There is no other way.

RANI: Yes, there is. Give me poison instead. Kill me right here. At least I'll be spared the humiliation. Won't the cobra bite me the moment I touch it? I'll die like your dog and your mongoose.

NAGA: No, it won't bite. Only, you must tell the truth.

RANI: What truth?

NAGA: The truth. Tell the truth while you are holding the cobra.

RANI: What truth? Shall I say my husband forgets his nights by next morning? Shall I say my husband brought a dog and a mongoose to kill this cobra, and yet suddenly he seems to know all about what the cobra will do or not do?

NAGA: Say anything. But you must speak the truth.

RANI: And if I lie?

NAGA: It will bite you.

RANI: God!

(*And then gently, almost menacingly.*)

And suppose what I think is the truth turns out to be false?

NAGA: I'm afraid it will have to bite you. What you think is not of any consequence. It must be the truth.

(*Anguished.*)

I can't help it, Rani. That's how it has always been. That's
how it will always be.

RANI: Oh, God!

NAGA: (*Gets up.*) All will be well, Rani. Don't worry. Your
husband will become your slave tomorrow. You will get all
you have ever wanted.

(*He turns to go.*)

RANI: Wait!

(*She suddenly runs to him and embraces him.*)

Please hold me tight. I'm afraid. Not of the cobra. Nor of
death! Of you. For you. You say you'll become my slave
tomorrow. That we will be together again. Why then does
your heart hammer so frantically? I had not even noticed it
until now. And now, why is it fluttering like a bird ambushed
in a net? Why this welcome to my child?

(*He slowly moves her away. Unable to look at him, unable
to keep quiet, she leans her forehead against the wall.*)

The night is almost over. You must go. But I know this is not
a morning like any before. Tomorrow won't be a day like any
other day. I don't want any tomorrows. Or days after. I want
this night to last forever. Remain unchanged. I mustn't let you
go. I must listen to my heart and hold you back. Take you
like a baby in my arms and keep you safe.

(*As she talks, Naga moves down the steps, turns into a
snake and goes away. She suddenly turns to him. He is not
there.*)

Listen. Please. Wait.

(*She rushes out. Runs to the front door. Lifts her hand to
open the latch. And freezes.*)

But the door . . . I had locked it from inside. And it is still
locked.

(*A new thought occurs to her. Almost unconsciously she runs
to the bathroom. Looks inside, it is empty.*)

Where are you? Where are you?

(*Sudden commotion. Crowds of villagers fill the stage from
all sides. The three Elders come and take their positions near
the ant-hill. The stage becomes the village square.*)

ELDER I: Dear child, we have done our best. But you refuse to

listen to us. We have no alternative now but to give in to
your demands.

ELDER II: It brings no credit to the village to have a husband
publicly question his wife's chastity. But Appanna here says:
Since the day of our wedding, I have not once touched my
wife or slept by her side. And yet she is pregnant. He has
registered the complaint, so we must judge its merits.

ELDER III: The traditional test in our Village Court has been to
take the oath while holding a red-hot iron in the hand.
Occasionally, the accused has chosen to plunge the hand in
boiling oil. But you insist on swearing by the King Cobra.
The news has spread and, as you can see, attracted large
crowds.

ELDER I: This Village Court has turned into a Country Fair.
Such curiosity is not healthy for the village, nor conducive to
justice.

ELDER III: Listen to us even now. If something goes wrong and
the Cobra bites you, not just your life but the life of the child
you carry will be in jeopardy. We risk the sin of killing your
unborn child.

ELDER II: To risk visiting such a sin on the whole village and the
Village Elders purely for a personal whim of yours is not
right. Think again. Listen to us. Desist from this stupidity.

ELDER I: We shall be content if you go through the ordeal of
the red-hot iron.

RANI: I am young and immature. I know nothing. But I ask
pardon of the Elders. I must swear by the King Cobra.

(*The Elders discuss animatedly among themselves.*)

ELDER I: All right. If you insist. Come now child. Truth shall
prevail. Come.

(*Rani steps up to the ant-hill. The crowds surge forward.
The Cobra rears its head out of the ant-hill. The crowd steps
back in terror. Even Rani is scared and runs back. The
Cobra waits, swaying its hood. Rani steps farther and farther
back. The Cobra goes back into the ant-hill.*)

ELDER II: Go on, child. Don't delay now.

RANI: I am scared. Please—if the Cobra bites me, what shall I
do? I am afraid—

(*Runs to Appanna.*)

Please, please, help me—

APPANNA: You whore—!

ELDER III: Appanna, there is no need to be vituperative. She
may have erred. But she is a child yet. Even we feel shaken
by the sight of the King Cobra. So her fright is quite
understandable.

ELDER I: If you are afraid, there is no need to go through with
the ordeal. Accept your guilt. We shall then go on to consider
the punishment.

RANI: But I have not done anything wrong. I am not guilty of
anything. What shall I plead guilty to?

ELDER II: (*Angry*) Listen to me. We have been patient until now
because of your youth. We have given in to your whims. But
you have tested us enough. Either confess or accept the
ordeal.

ELDER III: Remember, child, you have a choice of ordeals even
now.

RANI: (*Looking at the ant-hill*) Yes, I shall take my oath . . .
holding the red-hot iron.
    (*A roar of disappointment from the crowds. But the Elders
    are delighted.*)

APPANNA: This is ridiculous! You can't allow this harlot. . . .

ELDER I: Heaven be praised. It's a load off our conscience.

ELDER II: We have been saved.

ELDER III: Hurry up now. . . . Heat the iron rod. Quick!
    (*In all this confusion, Kurudavva enters calling her
    son.*)

KURUDAVVA: Kappanna, my son—Where are you? Can you hear
me?

RANI: Kurudavva—

KURUDAVVA: Has my son come here? Why is he teasing me like
this? Kappanna—

RANI: Kurudavva—
    (*Tries to rush after her but is stopped by Appanna.*)

APPANNA: Where do you think you are going?

ELDER I: Do you know that old woman? Don't you know she
has gone mad?

ELDER II: Her son disappeared a week ago.

ELDER III: We have all told her he is not in the village. But

she won't listen. Wanders around day and night calling
him—

KURUDAVVA: Kappanna, son—

RANI: (*Snarling at Appanna*) If you don't let go, I'll—

    (*Taken aback by her fury, Appanna lets her go.*)

ELDER III: Let her. The rod isn't hot yet.

RANI: (*Runs to Kurudavva*) Help me, Kurudavva. Help me,
please—

KURUDAVVA: Do you know where he is? He—

RANI: It's me. Rani. What shall I do? I don't know ...

KURUDAVVA: My Kappanna is gone. Melted away.

RANI: I am innocent, Kurudavva. I haven't done anything, what
shall I do?

KURUDAVVA: I woke up. It was midnight. I heard him panting.
He was not in his bed. He was standing up ... stiff ... like
a wooden pillar. Suddenly I knew. There was someone else in
the house. A third person ...

RANI: (*Mesmerized*) Who was it?

KURUDAVVA: If only I had my eyes! I would have seen her. I
would have recognized. But what can one do with these
pebbles? When he tried to tell me I didn't listen. I was deaf.
A temptress from beyond? A *yaksha* woman—Perhaps a
snake woman? But not a human being. No. What woman
would come inside our house at that hour? And how? She
wasn't even breathing. I shouted: 'Who are you? What do
you want from us? Go away!' Suddenly the door burst open.
The rushing wind shook the rafters. He slipped from my
hands and was gone. Never came back.

ELDER I: Rani—

KURUDAVVA: Now I wander about calling him. They tell me he
is not in the village. They think I am mad. I know he is not
here. I know he won't come back. But what can I do? How can
I sit in the house doing nothing? I must do something for him.

ELDER II: Rani—

KURUDAVVA: (*Getting up*) I must go. Look for my son. Can't
waste time like this—Kappanna, Son, it's your Mother. Don't
torment me now, child. ...

    (*Goes out. Rani stands staring in her direction. Then turns
to the Story.*)

RANI: Why should she suffer like this? Would sight have
helped? Do desires really reach out from some world beyond
right into our beds?
>   (*The crowd has become restive. So Rani's remaining
>   questions get lost in the increasing hubub. We only see her
>   addressing the Story, who does not answer.*)

ELDER I: Silence! Silence!
>   (*The crowd falls silent. Only the last part of Rani's dialogue
>   is heard.*)

RANI: (*To the Story*) Why should I let you push me around? Isn't
it better to accept the kiss of the Cobra and the dark silence
of the ant-hill?

ELDER II: Come, child. The iron rod is hot and ready.

RANI: No. I want the ordeal by the Cobra.
>   (*Goes to the ant-hill, plunges her hand into it and pulls the
>   Cobra out.*)

ELDER III: Be quick, now.

RANI: Since coming to this village, I have held by this hand, only
two. . . .

APPANNA: (*Triumphant.*) There. She admits it. Two, she says.
Two! Who are they?

RANI: My husband and . . .

APPANNA: And—say it, who else?

RANI: And this Cobra.
>   (*Suddenly words pour out.*)

Yes, my husband and this King Cobra. Except for these two,
I have not touched any one of the male sex. Nor have I
allowed any other male to touch me. If I lie, let the Cobra
bite me.
>   (*The Cobra slides up her shoulder and spreads its hood like
>   an umbrella over her head. The crowd gasps. The Cobra
>   sways its hood gently for a while, then becomes docile and
>   moves over her shoulder like a garland. Music fills the skies.
>   The light changes into a soft, luminous glow. Rani stares
>   uncomprehending as the Cobra slips back into the ant-hill.
>   There are hosannas and cheers from the crowd.*)

ELDER I: A miracle! A miracle!

ELDER II: She is not a woman. She is a Divine Being!

ELDER III: Indeed, a Goddess—!

(*They fall at her feet. The crowd surges forward to prostrate itself before her. Appanna stands, uncomprehending. The Elders shout, 'Palanquin! Music!' They lift her into the palanquin. Then, as an afterthought, Appanna is seated next to her. The couple is taken in procession to their house.*)

ELDER I: Appanna, your wife is not an ordinary woman. She is a goddess incarnate. Don't grieve that you judged her wrongly and treated her badly. That is how goddesses reveal themselves to the world. You were the chosen instrument for revealing her divinity.

ELDER II: Spend the rest of your life in her service. You need merit in ten past lives to be chosen for such holy duty.

ELDER III: Bless us, Mother. Bless our children.

(*All disperse, except Rani and Appanna. Appanna opens the lock on the door, throws it away. He goes in and sits, mortified, baffled. She comes and stands next to him. Long pause. Suddenly he falls at her feet.*)

APPANNA: Forgive me. I am a sinner. I was blind . . .

RANI: Hush, now!

(*She gently takes him in her arms. Music starts in the background and the words they speak to each other cannot be heard.*)

STORY: So Rani got everything she wished for, a devoted husband, a happy life. She even got a life-long servant to draw water for her house. For Appanna's concubine was present at the trial. When she saw Rani's glory, she felt ashamed of her sinful life and volunteered to do menial work in Rani's house. In due course, Rani gave birth to a beautiful child. A son. Rani lived happily ever after with her husband, child and servant.

(*Her last sentence is drowned in the hubub created by the Flames as they prepare to leave. 'That was a nice story!' 'Has it dawned yet?' 'I don't want to be late', 'Poor girl!'*)

MAN: (*Exasperated.*) These Flames are worse than my audience. Can't they wait till the story is over?

FLAME 1: But isn't it?

MAN: It can't be. No one will accept this ending.

STORY: But why not?

MAN: Too many loose ends. Take Kappanna's disappearance, for instance . . .

STORY: Oh, that is Kurudavva's story. If you are interested in that one, you may find her yet, meet her unexpectedly as you met me here, in some remote place. Even in the market place perhaps. Or someone in the audience may know. Or you can invent the missing details. That would be quite in order. I am only Rani's story.

MAN: Even then, the present ending just doesn't work.

STORY: And why not?

MAN: It is all right to say Rani lived happily ever after. But what about Appanna, her husband? As I see him, he will spend the rest of his days in misery.

(Appanna suddenly moves out of Rani's embrace. Speaks to himself.)

APPANNA: What am I to do? Is the whole world against me? Have I sinned so much that even Nature should laugh at me? I know I haven't slept with my wife. Let the world say what it likes. Let any miracle declare her a goddess. But *I* know! What sense am I to make of my life if that's worth nothing?

STORY: Well then, what about her?

(Rani does not speak but responds restlessly the Story's following dialogue.)

STORY: No two men make love alike. And that night of the Village Court, when her true husband climbed into bed with her, how could she fail to realize it was someone new? Even if she hadn't known earlier! When did the split take place? Every night this conundrum must have spread its hood out at her. Don't you think she must have cried out in anguish to know the answer?

MAN: So? The story is not over then?

STORY: When one says, 'And they lived happily ever after', all that is taken for granted. You sweep such headaches under the pillow and then press your head firmly down on them. It is something one has to live with, like a husband who snores, or a wife who is going bald.

(As the Story speaks, Rani and Appanna come together, smile, embrace and are plunged into darkness.)

MAN: But that ending lacks something. (*Remembering.*) Of
course, the Cobra!

STORY: Yes, the Cobra. One day the Cobra was sitting in its
ant-hill and it thought of Rani and said: 'Why should I not go
and take a look?'

(*During the above dialogue, the Cobra enters the house,
takes on his human form.*)

NAGA: Why should I not take a look? I have given her
everything. Her husband. Her child. Her home. Even her
maid. She must be happy. But I haven't seen her . . . . It is
night. She will be asleep. This is the right time to visit her.
The familiar road. At the familiar hour. (*Laughs.*) Hard to
believe now I was so besotted with her.

(*Goes into Rani's bedroom. Rani is sleeping next to her
husband, her head on his shoulders, her long loose tresses
hanging down from the edge of the cot. Her child is by her
side. There is a quiet smile of contentment on her face. Naga
looks at the group and recoils in sudden anguish. Covers his
face as though he cannot bear to see the scene.*)

NAGA: Rani! My queen! The fragrance of my nights! The
blossom of my dreams! In another man's arms? In another
man's bed? Does she curl around him as passionately every
night now? And dig her nails into his back? Bite his lips?
And here I am—a sloughed-off skin on the tip of a thorn. An
empty sac of snake-skin. No. I can't bear this. Someone must
die. Someone has to die. Why shouldn't I kill her? If I bury
my teeth into her breast now, she will be mine—mine forever.

(*Moves to her swiftly. But stops.*)

No, I can't. My love has stitched up my lips. Pulled out my
fangs. Torn out my sac of poison. Withdraw your veils of
light, Flames. Let my shame float away in the darkness. Don't
mock, gecko. Yes, this King Cobra is now no better than a
grass snake. Yes, that is it. A grass snake. A common reptile.
That's what I am, and I had forgotten that. I thought I could
become human. Turn into my own creation. No! Her thighs,
her bosom, her lips are for one who is forever a man. I shed
my own skin every season. How could I even hope to retain
the human form? For me—yes, only her long locks. Dark,
jet-black snake princesses.

(*Smells them.*)

They are like me. Reptilian. Cold. Long. They are right for
me. I shall summon my magical powers for the last time—to
become the size of her tresses. To become so thin, so small,
that I can hide in them, play with them, swim away in their
dark flow.

(*Presses her hair to his body.*)

Become their size now! Enter her tresses! Make love to them.
They have no sensation. They will not disturb her dreams.
But for you, that will suffice.

(*A beam of light on him. The rest is plunged into darkness.
Long dark hair appear to descend and cover him. He covers
himself and dances.*

*Finally, Naga ties a tress into a noose and places it around
his neck. The stage slowly becomes dark.*

Long silence.

Then Kurudavva's voice is heard in the distance.)

KURUDAVVA'S VOICE: Son! Where are you?

(*Lights come on. Rani, Appanna and child are sleeping.*)

KURUDAVVA'S VOICE: Kappanna—

(*Appanna sits up.*)

APPANNA: Yes?

RANI: (*Waking up*) What is it?

APPANNA: I thought I heard someone calling me.

KURUDAVVA'S VOICE: Kappanna! Where are you?

RANI: That poor soul: Kurudavva.

APPANNA: In my sleep, it sounded like—my Mother calling me—

RANI: Poor you!

(*Tries to sit up. Groans and clutches her hair.*)

APPANNA: What is it?

RANI: My head. It feels so heavy. Ahh! Please. Can you give me
a comb? My head weighs a ton. Let me comb my hair.

(*He gives her a comb. She tries to comb her hair, but cannot.
There is something caught up in her tresses.*)

(*To Appanna.*) Could you please?

APPANNA: Certainly.

(*He combs her hair. He has to struggle to get the comb
through. A dead cobra falls to the ground.*)

A cobra! Stay away!

(*They look at it from afar.*)

RANI: Oh! Poor thing, it is dead!

APPANNA: (*Examining the dead snake.*) You know—it seems to have got caught in your hair and strangled itself. Your long hair saved us, Rani. The Elders were right. You are no common person. You are a goddess.

RANI: We are not important. But our son is the blossom of our family. He has been saved. He has been given the gift of life by the Cobra, as by a father.

APPANNA: So?

RANI: (*Almost to herself.*) A cobra. It has to be ritually cremated. Can you grant me a favour?

APPANNA: Certainly.

RANI: When we cremate this snake, the fire should be lit by our son.

APPANNA: As you say.

RANI: And every year on this day, our son should perform the rituals to commemorate its death.

APPANNA: But aren't you going too far? I mean—that's done only for one's own father. And I am still alive.

RANI: Please don't say no.

APPANNA: Of course, there is no question of saying no. You are the goddess herself incarnate. Any wish of yours will be carried out.

(*He exits. She sits staring at the snake. Her eyes fill with tears. Music. She bows down to the dead snake, then picks it up and presses it to her cheeks. Freezes. It gets brighter, the Flames disappear, one by one. Story of course is gone.*)

FLAMES: Is it really over? ... Oh! What a lovely tale! etc.

MAN: (*Looks out.*) No sign of any light yet!

FLAME 3: Pity it has to end like that.

FLAME 2: These unhappy endings ...

FLAME 4: Why can't things end happily for a change?

MAN: But death! It's the only inescapable truth, you know.

FLAME 5: Don't be so pompous!

FLAME 1: (*Sharply.*) Then why are you running away from it?

FLAME 2: If darkness were the only option, we might as well have embraced it at home!

MAN: But—that's how the story is. That's how it ends. I'm not to blame.

FLAMES: Stop making excuses! ... The story may be over. But you are still here and still alive! ... Listen, we don't have much time left. ... Get on with it, for goodness' sake, etc.

MAN: All right! All right! Let me try.

(*The Flames rush back to their corners and wait expectantly. Rani and Appanna are sleeping, with the child next to them. Rani suddenly moans and sits up, holding her hair. Appanna wakes up.*)

APPANNA: What is it?

RANI: My head! It hurts—as though someone were pulling out my hair! Ahh! Please. Can you give me a comb? I can't bear the pain ...

(*He gives her a comb. She tries to comb her hair, but cannot. She gives the comb to Appanna.*)

Would you, please?

(*He takes the comb. Combs her hair. A live snake falls out of her hair and lies writhing on the floor.*)

APPANNA: A snake! Stay away! It's tiny, but it's a cobra, all right. And alive. How did it get into your hair? Thank god for your thick tresses. They saved you. Wait. We must kill it—

(*Backs away from the snake, then runs out shutting the bedroom door behind him. Searches for a stick in the kitchen. Rani watches the snake transfixed.*)

APPANNA: Isn't there a stick anywhere here?

RANI: (*Softly, to the Cobra.*) You? What are you doing here? He'll kill you. Go. Go away. No! Not that way. He's there. What shall we do? What shall we do? Why did you ever come in here, stupid? (*Suddenly.*) My hair! Of course. Come, quick. Climb into it.

(*She lets her hair down to the floor.*)

Quick now. Get it. Are you safely in there? Good. Now stay there. And lie still. You don't know how heavy you are. Let me get used to you, will you?

(*Appanna comes in with a stick.*)

It went that way—toward the bathroom.

(*Appanna rushes out of the bedroom, toward the bathroom, looking for the snake. Rani pats her hair.*)

This hair is the symbol of my wedded bliss. Live in there happily, for ever.

(*Lifts the baby up. Starts feeding it. She and Appanna freeze. It gets brighter. The flames disappear, one by one.*

We are back in the inner sanctum of the temple. The Man is sitting alone. He looks up. Sunlight pours in through the cracks in the temple roof. It is morning. The man vigorously stretches himself, bows to the audience and goes out.)